ROBIN HOOD

The Silver Arrow and the Slaves

LEVEL 2

SCHOLASTIC

Adapted by: Lynda Edwards

Fact Files written by: Jacquie Bloese

Publisher: Jacquie Bloese

Editor: Fiona Beddall

Designer: Mo Choy

Picture research: Emma Bree

Photo credits:

Cover and interior images © Tiger Aspect Productions 2006
Pages 50 & 51: Lebrecht Music and Arts Photo Library,
Detail Parenting/Alamy; Cinetext/Allstar. **Pages 52 & 53:**
Krause, Johansen/Archivo Iconografico, SA, Gianni Dagli
Orti/Corbis.

Published by Scholastic Ltd. 2008

Printed in China through Golden Cup Printing Services

Contents

Page

ROBIN

ROBIN HOOD was a rich man with a lot of land. He went away to fight for King Richard in the Middle East. When he returned, Sir Guy of Gisborne took his land. Now Robin lives with his men in Sherwood Forest. He takes money from rich people and gives it to the poor. He's the best archer in Nottingham.

MUCH was a poor man who worked for Robin. He went with him to the Middle East and he and Robin soon became good friends. Much is often frightened, usually hungry but always kind.

LITTLE JOHN lived in Sherwood Forest before Robin arrived. He is very big and strong – a useful man in a fight. He doesn't say a lot, but when he speaks, people listen.

4

HOOD

WILL SCARLETT is the youngest of Robin's men. He hates Gisborne and his boss, the Sheriff of Nottingham. Because of them, his mother is dead and his father has no right hand. He wants to help the people of Nottingham.

ALLAN A DALE

is Nottingham's greatest liar. Before he met Robin, he was only interested in himself. He was in big trouble with the Sheriff but Robin saved him. Now Allan uses his lies to help other people.

THE SHERIFF OF NOTTINGHAM

rules the town of Nottingham. He is clever but dangerous. He doesn't care about the poor people of Nottingham – and he hates Robin Hood. But will he ever catch him?

SIR GUY OF GISBORNE

takes orders from the Sheriff. He is quieter than his boss but just as dangerous. Like the Sheriff, he hates Robin Hood, but he is in love with Marian. He can't stay away from her.

MARIAN and Robin were in love before Robin went to the Middle East. Since then she has learnt to look after herself – and other people. She is beautiful and brave, but will she and Robin ever be together?

EDWARD is Marian's father, and he was once the Sheriff of Nottingham. He doesn't like the new Sheriff's rule, but what can he do? It is too dangerous to say anything. He wants to keep himself and his daughter safe.

DJAQ is a young slave with a secret.

ROWAN is a young boy from a poor family.

PLACES

Sherwood Forest:
A big area of land with lots of trees. The road to Nottingham goes through it, and Robin lives here with his men.

Nottingham Castle:
The home of the Sheriff. It is a strong, old building with lots of guards.

Treeton Mine:
People work in deep holes here to find iron ore. The mine makes a lot of money for the Sheriff and Gisborne, but it is very dangerous.

ROBIN HOOD

CHAPTER 1
Trouble at Treeton Mine

Every day at Treeton Mine was terrible, but today was worse than all the others. Clouds of black smoke covered the sky. Everywhere people lay hurt or dead. The terrible explosion at the mine was still sounding in people's ears.

Rowan found his father. He was sitting by the body of his uncle and crying.

'He's dead, Rowan. They're all dead.'

Rowan pointed at some men on horses. They were riding towards the mine. 'Look, Father. Here's Gisborne. Please tell him. The mine is too dangerous. We can't work here anymore.'

Sir Guy of Gisborne was dark and good-looking but his eyes were hard and cold. He got off his horse and looked at all the dead bodies. Rowan's father ran to him.

'We're not going to work in your mine anymore, Gisborne. We can't. It isn't safe. Make it safe and we'll go back to work.'

Gisborne was angry. 'You work when I tell you!' he shouted. 'Or do you want to join your brother?'

A man on a white horse was coming towards them. He had small, dark eyes and a strange smile. Everyone hated this man, the Sheriff of Nottingham, because he did terrible things to the poor. Only King Richard could stop him. But the king was fighting in the Crusades near Jerusalem and knew nothing of the troubles in England.

Slowly, the Sheriff got off his horse. 'I hope you're not giving these people a choice, Gisborne,' he said softly.

Gisborne looked at him. Then he took his knife and pushed it into the miner's body. Rowan couldn't believe it. His father fell onto the grass, dead.

'Very good,' said the Sheriff happily. Then he turned to the miners with a small, thin smile. 'Enjoy your free time. You've lost your jobs. Goodbye.' He started to walk away.

Gisborne followed him. He didn't understand. 'But we need miners. We need the iron ore from the mine,' he said.

The Sheriff smiled again. 'Don't worry, Gisborne. I have a plan! We will have miners. New miners.' He shouted at the men. '*They* will have work tomorrow. And you won't!'

Gisborne smiled too. 'Take away these bodies,' he said to the miners. 'You will not work. You will not get food. And I will kill anyone who tries to help you!'

* * *

Robin Hood was smiling. He was always happiest
when he was practising archery. It was quiet under the
trees and the light danced over the grass. His friends
Much, Allan, Will and Little John were all sleeping near
the fire. In his sleep, Much reached out his hand. Robin
took an arrow and carefully pointed it at Much. It flew
between Much's fingers.

Much woke up and looked angrily at Robin. 'I knew it!'
he said. 'You want to go to the silver arrow competition in
Nottingham.'

'No, I don't,' said Robin, and he shot another arrow into
a tree. He was easily the best archer in the area. 'I don't
care about the competition. Who wants to win a silver
arrow?!'

'Good,' said Much. 'Because we've got to find
food, cook it and eat it. We haven't got time to die in
Nottingham!'

* * *

Rowan stood outside the church with his mother and the families of the other dead miners. They were putting the bodies into big holes. It was raining and the sky was grey. Rowan held his mother. 'They will pay for this, Mother,' he said quietly.

Suddenly someone in dark clothes rode towards them. Who was it? Rowan couldn't see the person's face because it was covered.

The rider threw a bag of food on the grass.

'You mustn't help us!' cried Rowan. 'Gisborne will kill you. His men are everywhere.'

Without a word, the rider turned the horse and rode away.

* * *

Gisborne was waiting by the road. He saw everything.

As the rider was leaving the mine, he jumped out in front of him. The horse stopped suddenly and the rider fell onto the road. Gisborne pulled out his knife.

'You work for Robin Hood, don't you?' he shouted. 'Where is he?'

The rider said nothing.

'You'll talk to me soon,' continued Gisborne. 'Or do you want to die?'

Gisborne ran at the rider and cut his arm with his knife. Still the rider didn't speak.

'No voice! Not even "ouch!"?' laughed Gisborne.

Suddenly the rider hit Gisborne hard and he fell down. When he got up, he was too late. The rider was gone.

Gisborne was very, very angry. 'Does he think he can escape me?' he thought. 'He's made a big mistake! I'll find him. And then I'll kill him.'

* * *

Robin was shooting more arrows at the trees. Little John smiled. 'He really wants to win the silver arrow,' he thought.

Suddenly one of Robin's men appeared. It was Will.

'Quick, Robin! We've got one! A cart's fallen into our hole!'

'Let's go,' cried Robin and they all ran through the trees. The driver, a big fat man, was trying to push his cart out of the hole. He was red in the face and he was shouting angrily. Then he saw Robin and his men. They were all pointing arrows at him.

'Alright,' said the driver. He knew the stories about Robin Hood and his men. The poor people loved him but he was very unpopular with the rich. 'Here you are, Robin. I haven't got anything else.' And he threw a small bag onto the grass.

Much opened the bag. Inside there was a piece of glass.

'Very pretty,' he said. 'But we can't eat this!'

Then they heard a strange sound from the back of the cart.

'Horses?' asked Robin and he pulled back the cover. The back of the cart was full of men. They were locked in. Their faces were dirty and they looked tired and hungry. Robin looked into the big, brown eyes of a young boy.

'Take one,' said the driver and pointed at the men. 'They'll work for you. They understand a few words.'

For a moment Robin and his men just stood there in surprise.

Then Robin looked at the driver. 'Who are they? Where are you taking them?' he asked angrily.

'They're new workers for the Sheriff's mine,' the driver answered.

'I don't believe it,' said Much quietly. 'They're slaves. The Sheriff is buying people.'

CHAPTER 2
Robin's plan

In her room, Marian washed her arm. The water was red with blood. Suddenly she heard voices downstairs. Gisborne was there.

Marian's father, Edward, appeared at her door. He saw her arm. 'Are you hurt?' he asked.

Marian tried to smile. 'It's nothing,' she said. 'I cut it on a piece of wood. That's all.'

'Show me.' Her father touched her arm but Marian turned away.

'No, really. It's fine.' She covered the cut with her hand. 'What does Gisborne want?' she asked.

'I don't know,' said her father. They both went downstairs to the dining room.

Gisborne was waiting for them. He couldn't take his eyes off Marian as she came into the room. As usual, she was looking very beautiful with her long dark hair and big blue eyes. She was wonderful, he thought. But why did he always feel so uncomfortable when he was with her?

Marian hated Sir Guy but she had to be nice to him. Life was very difficult for people that he didn't like. 'How can we help you, Sir Guy?' she asked.

Gisborne looked at his hands and then he looked out of the window. 'Well, today I am going … you probably know …' He stopped for a moment. 'And perhaps you are also going … But I would like to ask you …' He stopped again.

'Going to …?' asked Marian.

'The Sheriff's fair,' Gisborne finally said. He looked down at his hands again. 'So, what's your answer?'

Marian smiled. 'I'm sorry, Sir Guy. I don't understand the question!'

Gisborne started to get angry. 'I'm inviting you to the fair. I'd like you to go with me.'

Marian tried to make an excuse. 'But I'm very tired, Sir Guy, and ...'

Gisborne stopped her. 'But will you come?' His eyes were hard now. Marian didn't have a choice.

'Good,' he continued. 'It will be an interesting day. The Sheriff is having an archery competition. The winner will get a silver arrow. Robin Hood will come and we will catch him at last.'

Marian smiled to herself. Robin was cleverer than the Sheriff. And he was a better man than Gisborne could ever be! Robin loved her and secretly she loved him too.

Gisborne was still talking. 'I nearly caught one of Robin's men today at the mine,' he said. 'He was giving food to the miners. He escaped but I'll know him again. I cut his arm.' Gisborne laughed and left the house.

Marian's father looked at her. 'It was you, wasn't it? You gave food to the miners.'

'Yes, Father. Robin Hood isn't the only one who helps the poor. We are rich. The miners needed food. I had to help them.'

Edward was frightened for his daughter. 'When did you start doing this?' he asked.

'Three years ago,' answered Marian.

$$* * *$$

Brooker, the cart driver, was eating and drinking with Robin's men. He was having a good time.

'What's going on, Robin?' asked Allan. 'It's not a party!'

Robin smiled. 'We're going to use Brooker to get to the mine. Then we're going to close it. That mine is dangerous. The Sheriff knows it and Gisborne knows it. And selling slaves is one of the worst things in the world. With Brooker's help, we can free the slaves *and* close the mine.'

He went to give some food to the slaves.

'Don't give them meat! They get too excited,' Brooker said loudly. 'And don't get close to them. There's a disease. Some of our men have died from it.'

Will's mouth fell open. 'They died?'

'A terrible way to die! One moment they were fine. Then, suddenly, blood was coming from their noses and they dropped down dead!'

Will's eyes were big. Brooker laughed. He was enjoying himself and the drink was good. 'You know, not long ago you could make good money from slaves. But then the Church stopped us selling Christians. It's lucky for me that King Richard likes fighting in the Middle East! These days most of my slaves are Turks.'

'Will, give the men in the cart some water,' said Robin.

Will didn't move. He looked frightened.

Robin laughed. 'There's no disease, Will. It's only a story. People will believe anything!'

Suddenly he stopped. His eyes were shining. 'Thanks, Will – you're brilliant!'

Robin spoke quietly to Little John. 'John, I have to look for something and I need some time. I want Brooker to go to sleep – understand?'

John smiled. He understood very well. His name, Little John, was a joke. He was really very big and strong. He walked towards Brooker and hit him hard. Brooker fell down and lay still.

* * *

Gisborne and the Sheriff were waiting for Brooker and the slaves at the empty mine. The women were still crying for their dead husbands. The Sheriff closed his eyes.

'That sound is terrible, Gisborne,' he said. 'It hurts my ears. Tell them that crying isn't allowed. And Gisborne,' he continued, 'never marry. Stay away from women! You can't live with voices like that.'

* * *

The men grouped around Robin as he told them his plan. He showed them a dark fruit that grew in Sherwood Forest.

'One of you is going to travel in the cart as a slave. He'll tell the guards at the mine about the terrible disease that Brooker talked about.' He smiled and looked at Much.

Much looked at Allan. 'Allan?'

'Alright. I'll do it,' said Allan. 'Do I have to eat this?' He looked at the strange fruit.

'When you are at the mine, put it in your mouth. It's safe but your mouth will go black. You'll look really ill. The guards will think you have the disease. They'll be frightened and run away.'

Much laughed. 'But no one will believe him!'

'People get frightened if they don't understand something,' said Robin. He looked at Will.

Will's face went red. 'I wasn't frightened!'

'No?' asked Robin with a kind smile.

Much was standing by the cart and he had the driver's glass in his hands. Suddenly the young boy slave reached out from the cart and took it. 'Hey!' shouted Much.

'It's mine!' cried the boy. His voice was high like a woman's.

Robin looked round. 'Ah!' he said. 'You speak English.'

Before the boy could answer, they heard the sound of wheels and horses on the road. Allan saw the people as they went past. He looked at Robin.

'You're not going to like this, Robin,' he said. He knew that Robin was in love with Marian. 'I think that was Marian with Gisborne's men. She's going to Nottingham. She's going to the fair – with Gisborne.'

CHAPTER 3
Djaq

Robin wasn't the only one with a good idea. While his friends were sleeping, Much visited the boy in the cart.

'We can get you out of here,' he said very quietly. 'It's easy.'

'You can unlock the cart,' said the boy angrily. 'That's easy.'

'No, my way is better. It's clever. The Church says that we can't buy and sell Christians. So you must say that you are a Christian. Then nobody can buy or sell you. See? Easy!' Much was pleased with himself.

'I must say that I don't believe in my god anymore?' asked the boy.

Much was excited. 'Yes! Say you believe in *our* god. Then the Sheriff can't buy you. You will be free and we can go home and eat.' He thought for a moment. 'But it's alright. Gods know everything. Your god will know that it's not true.'

The boy looked carefully at Much. He was thinking. 'So,' he said softly, 'if it's easy, you do it. Say you don't believe in your god.'

Much opened his mouth but he couldn't say the words. The boy laughed. 'See? You can't!'

'Yes I can!' Much looked round. Nobody was listening. 'I don't believe in God,' he said very quickly. 'See?'

As he walked away from the cart, Much looked quickly at the sky. 'I believe in you really,' he said quietly. The boy heard him and smiled.

* * *

The Sheriff was getting angry. The slaves were late.

'Where are they?' he shouted. 'I want to go to my fair.'

He looked at the guards. 'Come on!' he said to them. 'Do something! Walk up and down or something. I'm bored.'

The guards started to walk up and down in front of the Sheriff. He laughed like a little boy. 'Yes! Left, right, left, right, left …' He started to walk up and down too.

* * *

Robin and his men watched the Sheriff and the guards from the trees. It was funny but they didn't laugh. They were thinking about more important things.

Robin explained his plan carefully. 'Brooker will take the cart and the slaves to the mine. The Sheriff and Gisborne will leave for Nottingham and then Allan will become 'ill'. The guards will run away and we'll destroy the mine.'

He put his face close to Brooker's. 'Just take the Sheriff's money and go. Don't say anything about our plan or you'll die.'

Robin's voice was very quiet. Brooker believed him.

Suddenly they could smell smoke. People in the cart were shouting. The ropes of the cart were on fire!

The men ran quickly to stop the fire. Luckily no one was hurt.

Much looked at the sky. He was upset. 'It's my fault!' he thought. 'God, I'm so sorry! I believe in you really!'

Robin went to talk to the young boy in the cart. 'It was you, wasn't it? You started the fire with your glass. You were hoping to escape. What's your name?'

'Djaq,' the boy answered.

'Listen to me, Djaq,' continued Robin. 'We're trying to help you. We don't want to keep you here.'

Djaq looked at Robin angrily. 'That man took us from our country. Now you have taken us from him. You're the same!'

'Djaq, we will help you to escape,' said Robin. 'But leave now and the Sheriff will buy more slaves next month. We want to stop him. We want to close the mine.'

Djaq wasn't sure. 'How can you help us?' he asked.

'The Sheriff will pay money for you,' Robin explained. 'We'll give you the money. Then we'll help you to go home. Do you understand?'

Djaq said nothing.

Robin opened the door of the cart. 'If you don't want to help us, go now,' he said quietly. He pointed to the trees. Djaq looked at the open door. Was it safe to believe this man?

One of the other prisoners said something. Djaq put his face close to Robin's and smiled. 'He says that he wants to kill you!' he said softly.

Robin wasn't frightened. He understood Djaq's language. 'No! He says that he wants to wash. Off you go!' he said to the man with a laugh.

The slaves got off the cart. Only Djaq was still uncertain.

* * *

They were ready to go to the mine. But where was Djaq? Will went to look for him.

Finally he found him in the river. He was washing in the water and his clothes were lying on the grass.

Djaq heard Will behind him and turned round in surprise. He quickly collected the clothes and ran past Will angrily.

Will said nothing. He was too surprised. Djaq the slave boy was really a woman.

* * *

The Sheriff was shouting at Brooker. 'You're late! Show me my slaves.'

Brooker pulled the cover off the cart and the slaves came out. Allan was with them. He was wearing the same clothes as the other slaves but his face was covered.

The Sheriff looked at the slaves and smiled. 'Yes,' he thought, 'this was a good idea. Good, strong workers, and very cheap!' But then he saw Djaq and he stopped smiling.

'This one is very small.' He looked coldly at Brooker. 'I hope you don't want the same money for him.'

Brooker tried to smile. 'But …'

'If any of these men die before your next visit, you get less for them,' continued the Sheriff. He ordered Gisborne to pay Brooker. Then he smiled at the slaves and pointed to the entrance of the mine. 'Now,' he said to them, 'to work! Iron! Iron!' He walked away happily. Everything was going well. The mine was working again.

The guards shouted at the slaves and pushed them down into the mine. But when it was Allan's turn, he fell on the grass in front of the guard.

'Please!' he cried. 'Give me a different job! Please!'

The guard was surprised. 'You're English!'

'I ran away from the fighting against the Turks,' said Allan. 'There were a lot of us once, but the others died. There's a terrible disease. We English get it easily.'

'What disease?' asked the guard coldly.

'It's a horrible way to die! You fall down and blood comes out of your mouth and nose – thick, black blood. The smell is terrible …'

The guard pushed him with his foot. 'Get to work,' he shouted.

Allan looked down into the mine. It was cold and dark. 'Why did I agree to do this?' he asked himself as he climbed into the hole.

CHAPTER 4
A fantastic day?

Rowan hated Gisborne, his father's killer. He also hated himself. Why did he just stand there after the explosion? Why did he do nothing to save his father?

He felt terrible. There was only one thing that he could do. He had to kill Gisborne.

He left his mother and his home and he went to the mine. From the trees he saw Gisborne and the Sheriff with the slaves. It was time. Rowan started to move quietly towards Gisborne.

Suddenly a hand covered his mouth and pulled him back into the trees. He fell on his back. Robin was standing over him.

'Who are you?' he asked the boy.

Rowan was frightened but he spoke loudly. 'I'm Rowan, son of Dunne. Guy of Gisborne killed my father and I'm going to kill him!'

'No!' said Robin quietly. 'Killing Gisborne will change nothing. And one of my men is there. You will put him in danger.'

'But Gisborne must die!' cried Rowan. 'He has hurt so many people!'

Robin explained. 'Killing Gisborne or the Sheriff will not help anyone. The mine will stay open and more people will die in there. But there are other ways to hurt them. The iron ore from the mine makes them money. Without it, they will not be as strong.' His eyes were close to Rowan's. 'You can help us.'

* * *

Allan appeared suddenly at the entrance to the mine. He was shouting and crying. He pulled another man over the edge onto the grass. 'Help me!' he cried. 'God help us all. This man is dying.' The man just lay there. He didn't move.

The guard was frightened. The man looked very ill. 'Kill him!' he shouted.

'No! No!' cried Allan. 'You mustn't kill him! His blood will carry the disease. We will all die! Ahh!' Suddenly something black shot out of his mouth and showered the grass. The guards were scared and jumped back quickly. What was wrong with him? Was it the terrible disease?

They didn't wait to find out. They ran away as fast as they could.

For a moment the mine was empty and quiet. Then there was a great shout and Robin and his men ran out of the trees. 'Well done, Allan!' cried Robin. 'That was fantastic. Even I thought you were dying!'

Allan sat up and tried to clean the black juice from his face. 'What is this, Robin?'

'Don't worry – just don't eat it …' Robin said.

Allan looked up at Robin. 'It's a bit late to tell me that!' he said, frightened. He started to feel ill.

'You'll be fine,' said Robin. 'Now, men, find as much wood as you can. We're going to make a fire!'

* * *

Everyone was having a good time at the fair. Nottingham Castle was full of people. They were buying and selling things, and laughing and shouting together. There was even some dancing. The archery competition was just starting. Lots of people were coming to watch.

The Sheriff and Gisborne arrived from the mine and

joined Marian and her father. Marian smiled coolly at Gisborne. She wasn't happy to be there. But she needed Gisborne to like her. Then it was easier for her to help Robin and the people of Nottingham.

The Sheriff looked cross. He didn't like it when people were enjoying themselves. He preferred them to be unhappy. 'But perhaps we'll catch Robin Hood today,' he thought, and started to feel happier.

He looked at the people. 'Can you see the man who gave food to the miners?' he asked Gisborne.

'No. I know he's short. And he has a cut on his left arm,' said Gisborne quietly. 'I'll order all the men to wear nothing on their left arms. Then we can see.'

The Sheriff looked down at him. He wasn't pleased. 'I give the orders here,' he said coldly. 'Remember that.'

He turned to the people and lifted his hand. They were suddenly quiet.

'We have a little problem here,' he said. 'Some of you try to hide things. So there is going to be a new rule. This is to keep us all safe, you understand. Men must wear nothing on their left arms.' All the men started to show their left arms. The Sheriff smiled and sat down. 'Oh, and er … have a lovely fair,' he said.

* * *

Robin took the Sheriff's money from Brooker.

'Why can't I keep it?' asked the driver.

'You are a horrible man with a horrible business,' said Robin. 'You're lucky that we haven't killed you. Now go!'

Brooker shouted, 'You'll pay for this!' as he started along the road from the mine.

Much couldn't believe it. 'But Robin, he'll go to Nottingham and tell the Sheriff! Then they'll ride back here and …' Then his face cleared. 'Oh! I understand. They'll come here, and you'll go to the fair.'

Robin smiled. 'I know it's terrible to take Gisborne away from a beautiful woman!'

Rowan looked up. 'What beautiful woman?' he asked.

'Gisborne is in love. Her name is Marian,' Robin told Rowan. It was hard for him to say it. He knew that Marian didn't love Gisborne. But he still didn't like to think of her with him.

Robin turned to Djaq and gave her the Sheriff's money. He told her the way to a place where people could help her and her friends. The Turks were just leaving when Djaq saw Will. He was trying to start a fire but he wasn't doing a very good job.

Djaq smiled. 'I'll help you. This way is much better!'

She used her special glass and the fire jumped quickly to life. 'That was clever!' thought Will.

Robin was happy. His plan was working. Now he could go to Nottingham and win the silver arrow. He could also see Marian! He walked away from the mine with Allan and Little John.

'What a fantastic d…' he started to say.

But suddenly there was a loud crash. Robin turned quickly. Little John wasn't there. There was only a cloud of smoke and a big hole. It was an old entrance to the mine and Little John was at the bottom!

CHAPTER 5
At Nottingham Fair

The people of Nottingham were enjoying the archery competition. Some were pushing the people in front of them to get the best places. Everyone was shouting loudly for their favourites. But the Sheriff was bored. He was often bored when other people were happy.

'No sign of Robin Hood,' he said to Gisborne.

Gisborne was also bored. He was nearly asleep. 'It's too dangerous for him,' he answered. 'He won't come. He doesn't want to die!'

'Then I hope your man, Michael the Red, is the winner. I don't want to give away this silver arrow,' said the Sheriff.

Gisborne was surprised. 'But Sheriff ... the silver arrow will be mine, won't it?'

The Sheriff laughed. 'Gisborne, I'm not stupid! Either Robin Hood wins and I hang him. Then I keep the arrow. Or your man wins and he gives the arrow back to me.

Either way I don't lose anything. I win or I win! Understand?'

Gisborne looked away. 'I understand,' he said. Hoping for the silver arrow was stupid. The Sheriff always won!

∗ ∗ ∗

Robin and Much stood at the edge of the hole. They were shouting to Little John down the mine but he didn't answer. He didn't even move. He just lay there.

Rowan couldn't stand still. He wanted to destroy the mine before the Sheriff came back. He needed to hurt Gisborne badly. 'Hurry up!' he shouted at Robin. 'We've got to hurry and make the fires!'

Robin had more important things to worry about. 'We must rescue Little John first!' he said. 'I'm going down there to help him.'

Will held his arm. 'How are you going to help him, Robin? You're too big. The hole is small.'

'But we must do something!' cried Robin. 'Perhaps he's dying, Will! People die in mines all the time …' He was frightened for his friend.

Then Djaq spoke. 'Robin, I'll go down. I'm smaller than you.'

Robin looked at Djaq. 'But you're only a boy. You can't lift him. He's too heavy for you.'

'I can wake him up. Then he can lift himself. I can stop the blood too. My father was a doctor.' Djaq seemed very sure.

Robin took Djaq's hands. Perhaps this could work! 'Alright,' he said quietly. 'Try.'

Djaq smiled at Robin. 'Don't worry,' she said. Then she turned to the men. 'I need silver and water. Quickly!'

'Silver?!' asked Will.

'You can probably find some with the iron ore.'

Much ran to find the silver. 'It's all my fault!' he thought. 'God, I'm sorry! Get John out safely and I won't eat anything for three days. Three days, God! Believe me!'

Behind Robin, Rowan was very angry and upset. Why didn't they listen to him? They had to destroy the mine! That was the most important thing!

Suddenly he thought of an even better plan. 'Fine!' he shouted. 'Save Gisborne's mine and his money! I'm going to really hurt him. He took my father from me. So I'll take away the woman that he loves!'

But only Djaq heard him. She watched as the boy ran off down the road towards Nottingham.

* * *

Another archer in the competition shot an arrow but he wasn't very good. 'Where is Robin?' thought Marian. Perhaps he wasn't coming.

She was sitting uncomfortably next to Gisborne and cutting up some fruit.

'The next archer is my man, Marian. He's very good,' said Gisborne. He touched her arm. Then he looked at his hand. There was something wet on it – blood.

He looked up at Marian. Quickly she closed her hand round her fruit knife. She pushed in the knife to make a deep cut. It hurt, but her face showed nothing.

'I've cut myself,' she explained to Gisborne. She opened her hand. 'See? I've got some blood on my dress.'

Gisborne looked at the cut and then back at her face. He was quiet for a moment but then he turned back to the competition.

Marian closed her eyes. 'Thank you, God!' she thought.

* * *

Gisborne's man, Michael the Red, walked up to shoot his arrow. Everyone was quiet as he got ready. Just then there was a noise. A fat man with a hot, red face was pushing his way towards the Sheriff.

Michael the Red's arrow flew past his ear. The man turned in surprise. It was Brooker, the driver of the cart.

Brooker ran up to the Sheriff and Gisborne. He was very tired. It was difficult for him to speak.

He pointed towards the mine. The Sheriff smiled. Oh yes! This was more interesting!

'Does he want us to follow him?' he asked Gisborne.

Brooker was able to say two words. 'The mine!'

'Yes?' smiled the Sheriff. 'The mine?'

Brooker's mouth opened again. 'Robin Hood …'

'Yes. Robin Hood, the mine …?'

Finally Brooker spoke for the third time. 'Fire!' he said and then fell down heavily.

The Sheriff was still smiling. 'Mmm? Robin Hood, mine, fire …?' Then suddenly his face changed. Mine, fire, Robin Hood!! He got up quickly and his face was now very red.

'Guards! Guards!' he shouted. 'The mine!'

CHAPTER 6
'Can you smell smoke?'

The Sheriff and Gisborne rode through Sherwood Forest as fast as they could. They had to get to the mine before it was too late.

* * *

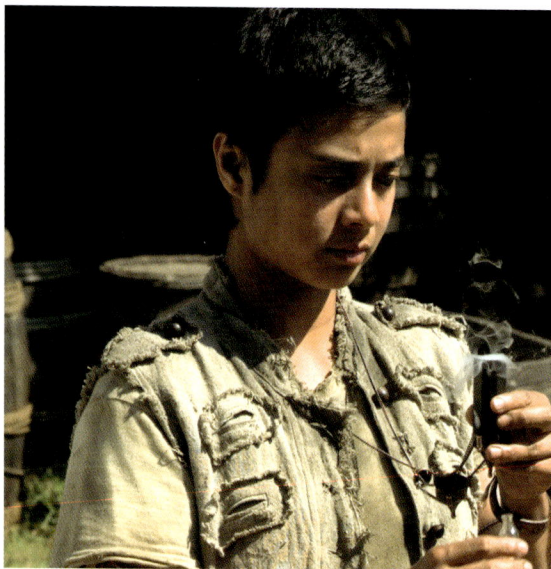

The men watched as Djaq put the special water in a small bottle. Blue smoke was coming from it and it had a strange smell. Allan gave Robin a frightened look. He wasn't sure about this.

'This boy and his bottle are our only hope,' said Robin quietly.

They put a thick rope round Djaq and dropped her slowly into the dark hole. Soon she was standing by Little John. The big man wasn't moving.

Allan looked down the road. 'The Sheriff is probably riding here right now,' he said to Robin. 'We have to hurry.'

Much spoke to God again. 'Please God! I won't eat anything for three days and three nights,' he said. 'Just help us, please!'

But there wasn't much time.

* * *

'Faster,' shouted the Sheriff, his eyes dark and angry. Gisborne said nothing. The horses rode faster through the trees.

* * *

Djaq put some of her special water on the cut on Little John's head. Then she held the bottle under John's nose. 'Come on, big man,' she said softly. 'Wake up.'

Little John opened his eyes. Then, slowly, he stood up.

'That's it!' Djaq said happily. 'Quick. Put this rope round you.'

She called to the men at the top. They stood in a line and pulled on the two ropes. It was hard work but soon Djaq's head appeared at the edge of the hole. She quickly climbed out.

Robin heard the sound of horses. He looked round and saw the Sheriff and Gisborne. They were coming down the road towards the mine.

'Quick!' he shouted. 'Pull harder! Come on, Little John!'

The men pushed their feet into the grass. They pulled as hard as they could.

'Robin!' shouted Will. 'They're here!'

The Sheriff and Gisborne rode into the mine with their guards.

With one last pull, Little John was finally out of the hole. He was safe.

Robin's men pulled out their knives and walked towards the men on horses. They were ready to fight.

But Robin pushed past them. 'Get Little John to the trees,' he said quietly. 'Leave this to me!'

He stood alone in front of the guards. They climbed off their horses. All except the Sheriff. He didn't like to fight. He preferred to watch.

Robin quickly put some arrows in the fire. Then he turned to fight the first guard. The guard lifted his knife, but Robin hit him hard. He fell on the grass.

'Where were your men, Gisborne?' The Sheriff was jumping up and down on his horse. 'Were they having lunch?!'

Robin took an arrow from the fire and shot it into one of the mine entrances. Two more guards ran up to him. He fought them both and then shot another fire arrow into the mine.

Fire was now coming out of the mine. 'The fire!' cried the Sheriff. 'Stop the fire!'

Robin laughed. 'Can anyone smell smoke?' he asked, and started to run to the trees.

Now the Sheriff's face was completely white. 'Stop the fire!' he shouted again at his men. 'Forget Robin Hood! Save the mine!'

Robin stopped and turned. He smiled at the Sheriff. '*Never* forget Robin Hood!' he said. He waved and ran into the trees.

* * *

Robin joined his men. 'Where is Rowan?' he asked.

'He'll be sorry that he didn't see the fire!' laughed Allan.

Djaq remembered Rowan's words. 'He's gone to hurt Gisborne,' she told Robin.

'But Gisborne's here,' said Robin. He could still hear the shouts of the Sheriff and Gisborne at the mine.

'His woman,' said Djaq. 'He's going to kill his woman.'

Robin didn't understand. 'But Gisborne hasn't got a woman.' Then Robin looked at Will and suddenly he understood Rowan's plan. His face went white. 'Marian!' he cried.

CHAPTER 7
The silver arrow

The Sheriff's guards threw water into the mine but they couldn't stop the fire. More explosions sent clouds of smoke up into the sky.

'Why didn't you have more guards here?!' the Sheriff shouted at Gisborne. He was very upset. It was the end of the mine. His mine, his iron ore, his money!

Gisborne tried to explain. 'But don't you remember? We thought that Robin was coming to the fair, to the archery competition …'

Both men stopped suddenly. Robin Hood! The fair! The archery competition! They ran to their horses again.

* * *

Rowan was at Nottingham Fair. He was in the archery competition and his arrow was pointing at Marian. 'Gisborne is going to lose her,' he thought, 'just like I lost my father.' He got ready to shoot. But at that moment, Marian moved.

Marian was tired of the competition. She decided to walk through the gardens of Nottingham Castle. It was quieter there.

Robin and his men arrived at the fair. They saw Rowan. He was walking towards the gardens.

'Follow him!' said Robin.

In the gardens, Marian heard someone behind her. She turned slowly. Rowan was pointing an arrow at her.

She stood very still. She was frightened but she didn't show it.

'It will be quick,' said Rowan. 'I shoot well.'

Marian looked into his eyes. 'You lost someone in the accident at the mine, didn't you?' She remembered the boy from the day when she brought the miners food.

Rowan was trying not to cry. 'He was my uncle. My father told him not to go down.'

Marian spoke softly. 'But he needed to work. He needed to buy food for his family.'

'Gisborne knew that it wasn't safe! He killed him!' Rowan shouted. 'And then he killed my father because he didn't want to work in the mine anymore.'

'Your father was a brave man,' said Marian in a quiet voice.

'I'm going to kill you. Gisborne too will lose someone that he loves!' Rowan's words were hard but he didn't sound sure.

Marian kept speaking. She couldn't hate this poor boy. 'Kill me and the Sheriff will kill you too. Then your mother will lose another man from her family. Think about her!'

There was no hope in Rowan's eyes. 'But I must do something.' He was crying now.

Marian tried to smile. 'Win the silver arrow! That will hurt Gisborne. Then use the silver to buy food for the miners.' She looked at him kindly. 'Or do you really want to kill a woman?'

Slowly she turned her back on Rowan and walked away. She closed her eyes and asked God for help. She waited to feel the arrow in her back.

But Rowan couldn't do it. He was crying hard now. He dropped his arrow.

At that moment Robin arrived. 'Marian!' he called.

Marian stopped. Now she knew she was safe. She looked at Robin but she didn't smile.

'You're late,' she said. 'Robin, this boy must win the silver arrow. Help him.' And she walked back to watch the competition.

* * *

A tall, slim archer won the archery competition. The people shouted and jumped up and down. But who was he? No one knew because his head was covered.

The Sheriff was happy at last. 'Brilliant!' he shouted. 'We've finally got Robin Hood! Guards!' But the archer ran away between the people at the fair.

The guards followed. Finally they caught him and pulled him in front of the Sheriff. The Sheriff laughed and uncovered the man's head. But it was Rowan, not Robin! The Sheriff was so surprised that for once he couldn't speak.

A small group of people left Nottingham Castle. One man's head was covered. It was Robin Hood and he was laughing.

* * *

After their busy day, Robin and his men were sitting and talking lazily under the trees. But poor Allan was feeling very ill. He couldn't eat anything.

'Don't worry,' said Robin. 'No food for one day and one night, and then you'll be fine.'

Much's eyes shone. 'Well, that's good, because there isn't much meat …'

Robin looked at him. 'But Much, you're not eating either. Three days without food, remember? God and I both heard you!'

Much looked away. He was trying to think of an excuse. He loved his food! 'Well,' he said, 'we're not really sure that God helped us. He didn't give us a sign, did he? So I'm going to build a fire and cook some food. And you can't stop me.' He got the wood ready for the fire.

Suddenly the fire started … without Much's help! 'Oh!' he cried, and sat back. Was this a sign?

Robin looked round. Something was shining in the trees – Djaq's glass.

Robin laughed. 'Come and join us, Djaq!' he called.

Djaq appeared from the trees. There was a big smile on her face. 'Join you for dinner, or for ever?'

Robin thought about the question. He liked Djaq a lot.

Will looked up. 'It's not safe for Djaq to join us,' he said quietly.

'Not safe for us, or not safe for him?' asked Robin.

Will looked away. 'Not safe for *her*,' he said.

'Djaq's a woman?!' Robin smiled. 'Well, I don't think that's a problem,' he said to Djaq. 'You saved Little John's life. Come on, men. Can a woman come and join us?'

'Yes, of course,' said Much. 'Can you …?'

'I cook very badly,' laughed Djaq, and Much's smile disappeared. But then he smiled again.

'Well, Djaq's glass started the fire, so it wasn't a sign from God. I can eat!' He reached for a piece of meat.

Suddenly there was a very loud crash. Much looked up at the black clouds in the sky and the food dropped from his hand.

'There's your sign, Much. Three days!' said Robin. Everyone laughed. Robin got up and took some meat from the fire. 'Now, who's hungry?'

Making ROBIN HOOD

Learning to fight at the Hood Academy

In 2006, Robin Hood arrived on TV in the UK. The programme-makers said it was 'Robin Hood for the 21st century'. It was cool, clever and funny. Soon, millions of people were watching it every week.

Made in Hungary

The programme-makers filmed in a forest outside Budapest in Hungary. The *Robin Hood* team was there for six months. When they weren't working, the actors loved the bars and clubs in Budapest. Their favourite bar was an Irish pub.

The Hood Academy

Before filming started, all the actors had to go to the 'Hood Academy' for two weeks. There, they learnt horse riding, archery and how to fight. The actors had to do all their own fighting and horse riding in the programme. Hungarian stuntmen only did the really dangerous stunts.

At first Jonas Armstrong (Robin Hood) didn't feel very comfortable on a horse – his legs hurt! But he soon became a good rider. For Lucy Griffiths (Marian), archery was the hardest thing. They had

FUNNY MOMENTS

"One of the team had to make a secret hole in the grass. Before filming started, he forgot it was there. He fell in head first. We could only see his feet! We all laughed so much."

Lucy Griffiths (Marian)

"My horse decided to run away – with me on it! People were shouting 'Stop, stop!' in English and Hungarian, but I couldn't do anything!"

Richard Armitage (Sir Guy)

competitions during their lessons. 'We all wanted to be the best!' remembers Gordon Kennedy (Little John). 'It was a true competition.'

Accidents

When the actors left the Hood Academy, filming started. There were lots of accidents. Keith Allen (the Sheriff of Nottingham) lost a tooth in a fight with Richard Armitage (Sir Guy). Harry Lloyd (Will Scarlett) cut his eye and had to go to hospital. And Sam Troughton (Much) fell off his horse – a lot!

Keith Allen (the Sheriff) at the Hood Academy

Would you like to watch *Robin Hood*? Why / Why not?

What do these words mean? You can use a dictionary.
programme century forest actor stunt/stuntman

ROBIN HOOD

Since the 1400s, there have been songs and stories about Robin Hood and his men. But who was he? Was he really the people's hero? Was he even a real person?

When?

People believe that Robin Hood lived in the late 1100s and early 1200s, when Richard I and then his brother John were King of England.

Where?

In most of the stories, Robin Hood lives in Sherwood Forest, near the town of Nottingham in the centre of England. The road from London to York ran through the forest. This road could be very dangerous. Sometimes, outlaws took money from travellers.

What is the legend?

The legend says that Sir Robin of Locksley fought for King Richard in the Middle East. When he came back to England, he lost his lands to the Sheriff of Nottingham. He chose to live as an outlaw in the forest with a group of men – Will Scarlett, Little John and others. He was quick, funny and a brilliant archer.

Who was the real Robin Hood?

No one knows for sure. We know that there was an outlaw called Robert Hod in 1225. There were a lot of people with the surname Hood, Hod and Hode in England at that time, and Robert and Robin were popular first names. This makes the search for the real Robin Hood very difficult!

An early picture of Robin Hood

~ the legend

The first stories

In the 1400s and 1500s, most people couldn't read and, of course, there was no TV. During the long winter evenings, people told stories and sang songs. The earliest stories about Robin Hood appeared around 1400.

In the first stories, Robin Hood wasn't a hero. He only thought about himself and didn't care about the poor.

The stories started to change in the 1500s. Then he became the people's hero. He took money from the rich and gave it to the poor.

The Robin Hood Fair, Nottingham

Robin Hood today

The outlaw of Sherwood Forest is as popular today as he was six hundred years ago. Every year, in Nottingham, there is a big Robin Hood fair. There are also many films and TV shows about him.

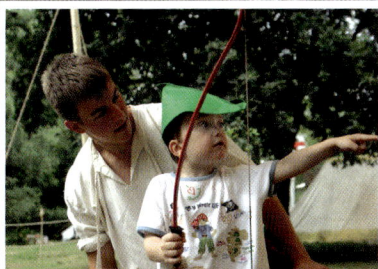

> Do you have any legends about heroes like Robin Hood in your country?

What do these words mean? You can use a dictionary.

legend   hero   forest   outlaw

Life in medieval

No school, and beer for breakfast! Was life in medieval England so bad?! Let's take a look ...

The rich and the poor

In the days of King Richard I, there was a big difference between the lives of the rich and the poor. A few important men – men like Sir Guy of Gisborne – owned all the land and even the poor people who lived on it. The poor weren't free to leave. They had to work for their owner and give him a lot of their food too.

Castles or huts?

The rich lived in castles or houses. They had tables, chairs and beds, but there was no glass in their windows!

The poor lived in small huts. There was usually only one room with a fire in the centre. Everyone slept on the floor. Sometimes their animals came in too!

What's for dinner?

Rich people ate – and drank – well. They ate lots of birds and other meat. The poor lived on bread, cheese and vegetables. Everyone drank 'ale' (a kind of beer) – even the children. In a year of bad weather, many of the poor died because there wasn't enough food.

THE CRUSADES

The Crusades were wars between the Christians and the Muslims in the Middle East. The first Crusade started in 1095, and the wars lasted almost 200 years. Christians from Europe wanted to take Jerusalem and the area around it from the Muslims. Both sides caught men and used them as slaves, like Djaq in 'The Silver Arrow and the Slaves'.

A Christian fighting in the Crusades

England

Work and play

The rich spent a lot of time hunting. They also had to fight for their king, in wars like the Crusades.

The poor worked on the land. They grew vegetables and kept animals. They sold their food in towns.

There weren't many schools, and most people couldn't read or write. Poor children started working with their parents at the age of seven or eight.

Life wasn't all work. There were holidays when the poor could enjoy themselves. They ate together,

A bird hunt

danced and watched fights between different animals. In the evenings, story-telling was popular. Sometimes towns had fairs, with archery competitions like the one in 'The Silver Arrow and the Slaves'.

A rich man with his workers

What was good about life in medieval England? What wasn't so good? How is it different to life today?

What do these words mean? You can use a dictionary.
medieval   beer   castle   hut
war   Muslim   hunting

53

CHAPTERS 1–2

Before you read

You can use your dictionary for these questions.

1 Can you name:
   a) something that is **silver**?
   b) something that you can find in a **mine**?
   c) the last **competition** that you were in?
   d) a **disease** that can kill people?
   e) something that people do at a **fair**?
   f) something that can make an **explosion**?
   g) something that can **cut** you?
   h) a famous **Christian** from the past?

2 Complete the sentences with these words.
   slave   cart   iron ore   guard   covered   ruled
   a) Horses can pull heavy things in a … .
   b) The men made knives from … .
   c) She … her face with her hands and cried.
   d) The … worked hard, but he hated his owner.
   e) King Richard … England at the time of Robin Hood.
   f) There was a … at the door. He didn't allow anyone inside the room.

3 Which two words are connected with **archery**?
   gun   shoot   arrow   boss

4 Look at 'People and Places' on pages 4–7. Which people are going to fight in this story, do you think?

After you read

5 Complete the sentences with the correct names.
   Gisborne   Will   Rowan   A rider   Allan   Edward
   a) …'s father dies at the mine.
   b) … kills a man with a knife.
   c) … gives food to the miners.
   d) … sees a cut on his daughter's arm.
   e) … gives Robin a good idea.
   f) … is going to go to the mine as a slave.

6 Answer the questions.
  a) Who is the rider that fought with Gisborne?
  b) What is Robin's plan?
  c) Would you like to live with Robin in Sherwood Forest? Why / Why not?

CHAPTERS 3–4

Before you read

7 Match the two halves of the sentences.
  a) That's the old building that the fire
  b) They pulled the boat with a thick
  c) Christians believe that there is only one

  i) god.
  ii) rope.
  iii) destroyed.

8 Guess the answers.
  a) Will Robin's plan work? Why / Why not?
  b) Will the Sheriff be happy when he sees his slaves? Why / Why not?

After you read

9 Are these sentences true or false? Correct the false sentences.
  a) Much tries to help the slave boy.
  b) The slave boy lies to Robin.
  c) Rowan goes to the mine to find Robin.
  d) The guards believe that Allan has a dangerous disease.
  e) Marian is enjoying herself at the fair.
  f) Djaq helps Will to make a fire.
  g) Will has an accident at the mine.

10 Choose the correct words to complete the sentences.
  a) The cart's **wheels** / **ropes** are on fire.
  b) Djaq is really a **woman** / **boy**.
  c) There is a **throwing** / **archery** competition at the fair.
  d) Gisborne is looking for a **tall** / **short** man.
  e) **Gisborne** / **The Sheriff** orders the men at the fair to show their left arms.
  f) Robin **wants** / **doesn't want** Brooker to go to the Sheriff.

11 Before Little John's accident, Robin is very happy. Why?

CHAPTERS 5–7

Before you read

12 Guess the answers to these questions.
   a) Someone goes down the hole and helps Little John. Who?
   b) What happens to the mine?
   c) Someone decides to shoot Marian. Who? Why? Does he kill her?
   d) Do Gisborne and the Sheriff find the rider who gave food to the miners?
   e) Who wins the archery competition?
   f) Who gets the silver arrow in the end?
   Now read chapters 5–7. Were your guesses right?

After you read

13 Put these parts of the story in order.
   a) Robin starts a fire in the mine.
   b) Gisborne sees that his hand has blood on it.
   c) Gisborne and the Sheriff arrive at the mine.
   d) Rowan points an arrow at Marian.
   e) Marian cuts her hand with a fruit knife.
   f) Little John gets out of the hole.

14 Correct these sentences.
   a) Djaq is a doctor.
   b) Robin saves Marian from Rowan.
   c) Much's fire starts as a sign from God.
   d) Djaq is going to stay in Sherwood Forest and cook for Robin and his men.

15 What do you think?
   a) How long will Much wait before he eats again?
   b) Will Djaq like her life in Sherwood Forest? Why / Why not?
   c) Gisborne and Robin both love Marian. Will she ever marry one of them? Which one? Why?
   d) Robin isn't trying to kill Gisborne and the Sheriff. Why not? Do you agree with Robin?
   e) Are there a lot of slaves in the world today? Can we do anything to stop the problem?

16 Who is your favourite person in the story? Why?